God Promised

Volume One

God Promised

Proclaiming the Word Over

Volume One

Worry, Anger, Fear, Anxiety, and Depression

Terri Flynn

God Promised
Proclaiming the Word Over

Worry, Anger, Fear, Anxiety, and Depression

Copyright © 2015 by Terri Flynn.

All rights reserved. No part of this book may be used or reproduced by any means, graphic, electronic, or mechanical, including photocopying, recording, taping or by any information storage retrieval system without the written permission of the author except in the case of brief quotations embodied in critical articles and reviews.

Because of the dynamic nature of the Internet, any web addresses or links contained in this book may have changed since publication and may no longer be valid. The views expressed in this work are solely those of the author.

Scriptures quotations taken from www.biblegateway.com

Scripture quotations marked ESV are from The Holy Bible, English Standard Version® copyright © 2001 by Crossway, a publishing ministry of Good News Publishers. Used by permission.

Scripture quotations marked GW are taken from GOD'S WORD®, © 1995 God's Word to the Nations. Baker Publishing Group. Used by permission.

Scripture quotations marked KJV are taken from the King James Version of the Bible, Public domain.

Scripture quotations marked NASB are taken from the NEW AMERICAN STANDARD BIBLE®, Copyright © 1960,1962,1963,1968,1971,1972,1973,1975,1977,1995 by The Lockman Foundation. Used by permission.

Scripture quotations marked NIV are from the Holy Bible, New International Version. Copyright © 1973, 1978, 1884, International Bible Society. Used by permission.

Scripture quotations marked NKJV are taken from the New King James Version®. Copyright © 1982 by Thomas Nelson, Inc. Used by permission. All rights reserved.

Scripture quotations marked NLT are from the Holy Bible, New Living Translation copyright © 1996, 2004, 2007, 2013 by Tyndale House Foundation. Used by permission of Tyndale House Publishers Inc., Carol Stream, Illinois 60188. All rights reserved.

Scripture taken from The Message. Copyright © 1993, 1994, 1995, 1996, 2000, 2001, 2002. NavPress Publishing Group. Used by permission.

Scripture quotations marked HCSB are taken from the Holman Christian Standard Bible®, Copyright © 1999, 2000, 2002, 2003, 2009 by Holman Bible Publishers. Used by permission.

Scripture quotations marked GNT are from the Good News Translation® (Today's English Version, Second Edition) Copyright © 1992 American Bible Society. All rights reserved.

Scripture quotations marked NCV are from the New Century Version®. Copyright © 2005 by Thomas Nelson, Inc. Used by permission. All rights reserved.

Scripture quotations marked NRSV are from the New Revised Standard Version Bible, copyright © 1989 the Division of Christian Education of the National Council of the Churches of Christ in the United States of America. Used by permission. All rights reserved.

Scripture quotations marked NET are from the New English Translation, NET Bible® copyright ©1996-2006 by Biblical Studies Press, L.L.C. Scripture quoted by per

Library of Congress Cataloging-in-Publication Data: An application to register this book for cataloging has been submitted to the Library of Congress.

ISBN: 978-1500715571 Soft cover

ISBN: 1500715573 E-book

https://www.createspace.com/4926657

Printed in the United States of America

Dedication

I would like to dedicate this book to my niece Rachael Pearl. When I started writing this book I had no idea that you were wrestling with anxiety and depression, but God knew. I suppose that is why volume one is addressing those issues. Remember as you fight this battle, you are simply carrying your cross; so pick up your sword and proclaim what Jesus promised.

The idea for this book series was suggested by my husband, Sean who asked me to write a book about God's Promises. Thank you from the bottom of my heart for the support and encouragement you continuously give me.

I also want to thank my dear friends Debra Ferrell and Kay White for their help with editing, proofreading, and formatting this book; it is greatly appreciated.

Contents

Dedication	vii
Preface	ix
Using this Book	xii
God Keeps His Promises	xv
Chapter 1 - Worry	1
Prayer for Worry	3
Scriptures about Worry	4
Chapter 2 - Anger	10
Prayer for Anger	13
Scriptures about Anger	14
Chapter 3 - Fear	19
Prayer for Fear	21
Scriptures about Fear	22
Chapter 4 - Anxiety	28
Prayer for Anxiety	32
Scriptures about Anxiety	33
Chapter 5 - Depression	39
Prayer for Depression	42
Scriptures about Depression	43
Prayer of Salvation	49
About the Author	51

Preface

Dear Readers,

Many years ago I started searching the Scriptures to see what the Bible had to say about the heartache and disappointments I was feeling. I had just gone through a divorce and my life was in chaos. I discovered then that proclaiming the Word of God helped me live beyond my feelings. Once I started thoroughly studying the Scriptures, I realized that feelings will come and go, that we will all endure loss, and that people will hurt us; sadly we can't escape these but we can choose to live by God's Word and not, by our feelings.

The first step to living by God's Word is to be knowledgeable about what He says. God's Word contains thousands of promises waiting to be claimed. However, we often miss the promises God has made to us because we simply don't know where to find them in the Bible. That is why I wrote this series, *God Promised Proclaiming the Word Over.* The first book of the series contains Scriptures about *Worry, Anger, Fear, Anxiety, and Depression.*

This collection of faith building Scripture is a powerful resource. It is designed to bring encouragement and calm an anxious mind. When we find the faith to speak the Word of God over our situation, then He will heal our broken hearts and bind up our wounds. God wants us full of joy, not full of sorrow; through His Word we obtain the power to heal our body and mind. Jesus destroyed the power of the devil and He gave us the authority over all his assaults.

The Word of God has defeated Satan's grip on our physical and emotional health. It's time for us to recognize that our healing has already been purchased at the Cross and, that the truth of God's Word makes us free from the Enemies grip.

The power and authority that we have been given in Jesus' name also gives us the right to choose what we will or will not allow in our lives. Jesus told us that we have the right, power, and permission to bind what-so-ever on earth in His name. Jesus' name carries all the authority of Jesus Himself. And when we proclaim the Word of God in Jesus' name with that authority we can speak to all of our problems.

We may not look healed. We may not feel healed but Jesus Himself carried our sins in His body to the cross and it is by His wounds that we have been healed. With God's Word as our foundation and by the authority of Jesus' name; we can tell the mountains to be removed. Remember that our mountain is anything that is hindering God's will from being done in our life. It could be worry, depression, fear, anxiety, stress heartbreak or any problem that is in opposition to God's will.

This book has been prepared to assist those who are seeking God for an answer. It will help you developed your faith and give you a better awareness of the promises of God. The Bible is our instruction manual for life and by proclaiming God's Word back to Him; we show Him we agree with Him.

These are a few reasons you will find *God Promised Proclaiming the Word Over* valuable.

Volume one offers Scripture on Worry, Anger, Fear, Anxiety, and Depression.

This series of books will motivate you to proclaim the Word of God over your life.

Each section includes information about a particular subject; a Scripture based prayer for that specific need, and Scriptures dealing with that particular situation.

It will encourage you to develop a closer relationship with God as you proclaim His Word back to Him.

Using this Book

The goal of this book is not just to emphasis the importance of proclaiming God's Word back to Him, but also to help you quickly find and apply God's Word to your life. If you are ready for a change, *God Promised Proclaiming the Word* will help you move forward by inspiring you to trust in and speak His promises over your struggles.

Our entire Christian belief system is based on us trusting the promises of God. When life is calm it is a lot simpler to say that we trust God. However, when everything is in chaos our words may not display this belief. The storms of life can crush our way of thinking and our faith will be tested in tough times. When a storm rages into our life, our Heavenly Father has already planned how to turn destruction into good.

Life is a journey of problem-solving opportunities and the challenges that we encounter can sometimes bring a feeling of anxiety or fear. Depending on how we confront those challenges, they will either defeat us or increase our Godly character.

God uses difficult times to steep us, just like a teabag. If we want to know what's inside of a teabag, we just need to drop it into hot water; then what is on the inside will come out. The longer it steeps the stronger it becomes. We have to believe that God knows what He is doing while we are going through the steeping process.

There is a mighty strength that comes from the knowledge that you and I are sons and daughters of God. That is why we have the right and authority to resist the spirits of worry, anger, fear, anxiety, and depression in the name of Jesus. God's promises have not given us a spirit of fearfulness, but one of power, love, and sound mind. God's Word gives us a remedy to our anxious concerns. When we have the knowledge of God's Word and we allow it to influence our life there is no reason to fear.

This book provides a Biblical foundation to help you experience spiritual break through. When times are challenging we need to remind ourselves that no pain comes without a purpose and everything in life is temporary. Besides, worrying or complaining about yesterday and today won't change tomorrow. Dealing with our past is something that we will all have to eventually do. When we hold on to resentment, anger, and problems from before, chances are high that the shadow of our past will hold our future hostage. Make the decision to not let the shadows of the past cast a shadow on a bright future, one full of possibilities. When things are going wrong, it's hard to be aware of what is going right but there is no better way to change a circumstance than proclaiming God's Word over it.

This book is comprised of Scriptures categorizing the promises of God by groups and themes. There are 5 chapters; each of these chapters follows a similar pattern and consists of three sections.

Each chapter is dedicated to a specific topic; which includes a Scripture based prayer, and Scriptures to proclaim.

Section 1 provides an explanation on the subject covered in that chapter.

Section 2 contains Scripture based prayer on the subject.

Section 3 includes a list of Scriptures which identify the promises that God has made on the subject.

Use these Scripture based prayers to talk to God while you use your authority in the name of Jesus. I hope that reading this book deepens your understanding of the Word of God and His promises to you, as well as offer you comfort in your journey to peace and healing. As you meditate on these Scriptures, allow them to enter your heart and proclaim them out loud.

God Keeps His Promises

God continuously keeps His promises

"For all the promises of God in Him are Yes, and in Him Amen, to the glory of God through us."   2 Corinthians 1:19-20 NKJV

God will never break His promises

"No, I will not break my covenant; I will not take back one word of what I said." Psalm 89:34 TLB

God has promised us freedom from fear

"I sought the Lord, and he answered me, and delivered me from all my fears." Psalm 34:4 RSV

God has promised us peace

"You will keep in perfect peace all who trust in You, all whose thoughts are fixed on You! God has promised victory over temptations." Isaiah 26:3 NLT

God has promise us health

"For I will restore health to you and heal you of your wounds,' says the Lord." Jeremiah 30:17 NKJV

God has promised us safety

"He will cover you with his feathers. He will shelter you with his wings. His faithful promises are your armor and protection. Do not be afraid of the terrors of the night, nor the arrow that flies in the day. Do not dread the disease that stalks in darkness, nor the disaster that strikes at midday." Psalm 91:4-6 NLT

God has promised us joy

"He will wipe away every tear from their eyes. There will be no more death, sadness, crying, or pain. All the old ways are gone." Revelation 21:4 ERV

God does not hold back anything that is good for us

"For the Lord God is our sun and our shield. He gives us grace and glory. The Lord will withhold no good thing from those who do what is right." Psalm 84:11 NLV

Chapter 1

Worry

Worrying is an area that many Christians struggle with and is harmful to us in many ways. Worrying adversely affects our lives, it can damage our well-being, consume our thoughts, interrupt our productivity, negatively affect the way we treat people, and weaken our faith. It can also become an emotional overload that causes us to develop physical illness. Worrying can cause sleep deprivation, ulcers, headaches, or high blood pressure. The weight of worry drags us down but God's Word lightens our day.

Worrying puts our focus in the wrong direction but when we keep our eyes focused on God we truly have nothing to worry about. God has a glorious plan for our lives and part of that plan includes peace. God's Word promises in Philippians 4:7, *Then you will experience God's peace, which exceeds anything we can understand. His peace will guard your hearts and minds as you live in Christ Jesus.*

Even in challenging times we can put our trust in the Lord and focus on His promises. We can have faith that God will take care of our every need. When we give all our worries and cares to Him, He is faithful to take them from us.

Worrying is the opposite of trusting God because when we worry we are focusing on the immediate problem instead of the promises of God. The energy spent on worrying can be put to much better use in prayer. We can trust God to do what's best for us. When we have a positive attitude and keep our faith in God we can't be defeated. Worrying won't help us solve a problem or bring about a solution; so we need to stop wasting our time and energy on it. God's Word tells us in Luke 12:25-26, *Can all your worries add a single moment to your life? And if worry can't accomplish a little thing like that, what's the use of worrying over bigger things?*

Worrying is a waste of precious time. I don't know about you but I don't have time to waste these days. I am sure that over my lifetime, worrying accounts for hours and hours of valuable time and the time I've wasted on worrying can never be reclaimed.

When we start to feel worried reading Scriptures and proclaiming Gods promises over our concerns is the best answer. God has asked us not to worry but to trust Him completely. God's Word tells us in Philippians 4:6, *Don't worry about anything, but pray and ask God for everything you need, always giving thanks for what you have.* God has already promised to give us all that we need, all we need to do is ask Him, and thank Him for all that He has done and all that He will do for us.

I can't think of anything more destructive than worry, but on the other hand, I can't think of anything more constructive than prayer. When you are tempted to worry, pray instead. Use these Scriptures about worry to help during stressful times; they are your reassurance of God's promises.

Prayer for Worry

Heavenly Father, I am so grateful that I can cast all my cares on to You and You will sustain me; because You will never let the righteous be shaken. I am convinced that Your peace, which goes beyond anything I can imagine, will guard my thoughts and emotions through Christ Jesus. I declare, that I will not give in to worry or anger because it only leads to trouble. I am convinced that whoever listens to You will live without worry

Holy Spirit, remind me that when I need the Lord, when I look for Him, and I call out to Him that He will hear me and responded. I declare, I will give all my worries and cares to God, because He cares about me.

Dear Lord, I confess that I will not worry because You are with me. I don't need to be afraid because You are my Lord, You make me strong, and You help me. You support me with Your right hand that saves me. I declare, that I will lift up my eyes to the hills where my help come from. I am certain that my help comes from You, who made heaven and earth. I declare that all my worries cannot add a single moment to my life, so I will not worry about tomorrow, for tomorrow will worry about itself and today has enough trouble of its own. and will be free from the dread of disaster.

In the mighty name of Jesus and by the authority He has given to me I command the spirit of worry to release me. Amen.

Scriptures about Worry

"But whoever listens to me will live without worry and will be free from the dread of disaster." Proverbs 1:33 GW

"Don't give in to worry or anger; it only leads to trouble." Psalm 37:8 GNT

"Why do you worry about clothing? Think about how the flowers of the field grow; they do not work or spin." Matthew 6:28 NET

"Cast your cares on the Lord and He will sustain you; He will never let the righteous be shaken." Psalm 55:22 NIV

"Never worry about anything. But in every situation let God know what you need in prayers and requests while giving thanks. 7 Then God's peace, which goes beyond anything we can imagine, will guard your thoughts and emotions through Christ Jesus." Philippians 4:6-7 GW

"And do not seek what you will eat and what you will drink, and do not keep worrying." Luke 12:29 NASB

"Don't let evil people worry you; don't be envious of them." Proverbs 24:19 GNT

"So I tell you to stop worrying about what you will eat, drink, or wear. Isn't life more than food and the body more than clothes? 26 "Look at the birds. They don't plant, harvest, or gather the harvest into barns. Yet, your heavenly Father feeds them. Aren't you worth more than they?" Matthew 6:25-27 GW

"Keep me as the apple of Your eye; hide me in the shadow of Your wings." Psalm 17:8 NIV

"So don't ever worry about tomorrow. After all, tomorrow will worry about itself. Each day has enough trouble of its own." Matthew 6:34 GW

"Then, turning to His disciples, Jesus said, "That is why I tell you not to worry about everyday life—whether you have enough food to eat or enough clothes to wear." Luke 12:22 NLT

"For the Spirit God gave us does not make us timid, but gives us power, love and self-discipline." 2 Timothy 1:7 NIV

"Can any of you add an hour to your life by worrying?" Luke 12:25 GW

"So don't worry in advance about how to answer the charges against you." Luke 21:14 NLT

"But even if you suffer for doing what is right, God will reward you for it. So don't worry or be afraid of their threats." 1 Peter 3:14 NLT

"So what should we say about all of this? If God is on our side, then tell me: whom should we fear?" Romans 8:31 VOICE

"I have set the Lord continually before me; Because He is at my right hand, I will not be shaken." Psalm 16:8 NASB

"He will cover you with His feathers, and under His wings you will find refuge; His faithfulness will be your shield and rampart." Psalm 91:4 NIV

"So don't worry, because I am with you. Don't be afraid, because I am your God. I will make you strong and will help you; I will support you with my right hand that saves you." Isaiah 41:10 NCV

"And we know that in all things God works for the good of those who love Him, who have been called according to His purpose." Romans 8:28 NIV

"The Eternal is the source of my strength and the shield that guards me. When I learn to rest and truly trust Him, He sends His help. This is why my heart is singing! I open my mouth to praise Him, and thankfulness rises as song." Psalm 28:7 VOICE

"I lift up my eyes to the hills where will my help come? 2 My help comes from the Lord, who made heaven and earth." Psalm 121:1-2 NRSV

"They will have no fear of bad news; their hearts are steadfast, trusting in the Lord." Psalm 112:7 NIV

"I say this because I know what I am planning for you," says the Lord. "I have good plans for you, not plans to hurt you. I will give you hope and a good future." Jeremiah 29:11 NCV

"Trust in the LORD with all your heart and lean not on your own understanding." Proverbs 3:5 NIV

"I have fought the good fight, I have finished the race, and I have kept the faith." 2 Timothy 4:7 NIV

"God is our shelter and our strength. When troubles seem near, God is nearer, and He's ready to help. So why run and hide?" Psalm 46:1 VOICE

"Let not your heart be troubled; you believe in God, believe also in Me." John 14:1 NKJV

"When struck by fear, I let go, depending securely upon You alone." Psalm 56:3 VOICE

"Be strong and courageous. Do not be afraid or terrified because of them, for the Lord your God goes with you; He will never leave you nor forsake you." Deuteronomy 31:6 NIV

"When I needed the Lord, I looked for Him; I called out to Him, and He heard me and responded. He came and rescued me from everything that made me so afraid." Psalm 34:4-7 VOICE

"Give all your worries and cares to God, for he cares about you. Stay alert! Watch out for your great enemy, the devil. He prowls around like a roaring lion, looking for someone to devour." 1 Peter 5:7-8 NLT

"As for God, His way is perfect: The Lord's Word is flawless; He shields all who take refuge in Him." 2 Samuel 22:31 NIV

"Then Jesus said, "Come to me, all of you who are weary and carry heavy burdens, and I will give you rest." Matthew 11:28-30 NLT

*"In my desperation I prayed, and the L*ORD* listened; He saved me from all my troubles." Psalm 34:6 NLT*

"He alone is my rock and the One Who saves me. He is my strong place. I will not be shaken." Psalm 62:6 NLV

"The Lord is my strength and my defense; He has become my salvation. He is my God, and I will praise Him, my father's God, and I will exalt Him." Exodus 15:2 NIV

"I am leaving you with a gift—peace of mind and heart. And the peace I give is a gift the world cannot give. So don't be troubled or afraid." John 14:27 NLT

"My body and my mind may become weak, but God is my strength. He is mine forever." Psalm 73:26 NCV

"Because of the Lord's s great love we are not consumed, for His compassions never fail. They are new every morning; great is Your faithfulness." Lamentations 3:22-23 NIV

"So what should we say about all of this? If God is on our side, then tell me: whom should we fear?" Romans 8:31 VOICE

"Are God's consolations not enough for you, words spoken gently to you?" Job 15:11 NIV

"The righteous cry out, and the Lord hears them; He delivers them from all their troubles. The Lord is close to

the brokenhearted and saves those who are crushed in spirit. The righteous person may have many troubles, but the Lord delivers him from them all." Psalm34:17-19 NIV

"For the angel of the Lord is a guard; He surrounds and defends all who fear Him." Psalm 34:7 NLT

"Guide me in your truth and teach me, for you are God my Savior, and my hope is in you all day long." Psalm 25:5 NIV

"For he shall be like a tree planted by the waters, Which spreads out its roots by the river, And will not fear when heat comes; But its leaf will be green, and will not be anxious in the year of drought, nor will cease from yielding fruit." Jeremiah 17:8 NKJV

"For the Word of the Lord is right and true; He is faithful in all He does. The Lord loves righteousness and justice; the earth is full of His unfailing love." Psalm 33:4-5 NIV

"Everything God does is perfect; the promise of the Eternal rings true; He stands as a shield for all who hide in Him." Psalm 18:30 VOICE

Chapter 2

Anger

Anger is an emotional response related to our perception of having been offended, hurt, or denied. We've all struggles with anger from time to time, whether as a passing frustration or as a tangible rage. Getting angry is very easy to me these days; a week doesn't go by that I don't get upset over at least a few things. So it made me wonder if getting angry is a sin. As I look through the Bible I found many passages on anger, I found that Moses, Jonah, Jeremiah and even Jesus and God got angry at times.

It's normal to feel angry when we've been mistreated or wronged. The feeling isn't the problem; it's what we do with it that is. So often we tend to defend and hold onto anger. If we don't keep anger under control it can become a destructive emotion taking captive our thoughts, our physical health, and it can also harm others. Anger is often displayed by a spirit of discontentment, resentment, and sometimes turns in to hostility. It can start with a feeling then it may be communicated in words or actions.

Many times the consequences of out-of-control anger are long-lasting. Spiteful speech is a common characteristic of anger, we need to learn how to speak the truth in love and use our words to build others up, not allow unpleasant or hurtful words to come from our lips.

Often one of the core roots of anger can come from our family. They are the closest to us and the ones that can disappoint us or upset us the easiest. Since we learn from our parents or guardians we often acquire the same behavior passing it on to their children. That is why so often angry people come from an angry upbringing. Handling anger is an important life skill but not handling anger properly can hinder and tear apart relationships. Therefore, we must accept responsibility for our part and work out the problem.

The first negative emotion mentioned in the Bible was anger. The Bible tells us in Genesis 4:4, *But He didn't approve of Cain and his offering." So Cain became very angry and was disappointed.* Cain's jealousy developed into anger and he killed his brother Abel because God had rejected his offering and accepted his brothers offering. When our expectations of God or others are not met, many peoples' first response is to become angry.

One sign that anger has turned to sin is when, instead of dealing with the problem, we attack the people involved. Also anger can become sinful when it is allowed to boil over, when it is inspired by pride, when we hold a grudge, when we keep it inside, or when it becomes a situation in which people are injured.

God's Word provides principles on how to manage our anger and how to overcome sinful anger. In the New Testament two Greek words are translated as anger, "orge" means passion or energy and "thuos" means agitated or boiling. Biblical anger is God given passionate energy intended to help us solve problems. Passionate energy is called righteous indignation. This type of anger God approves, for that reason anger is not always sin.

Throughout the Bible we are told how to handle anger in a godly manner. The Bible tells us in Ephesians 4:26, *Be angry without sinning. Don't go to bed angry.* This scripture is teaching us two things about anger; first to beware of sinning; we can do that by keeping our anger clear of bitterness, spite, and evil feelings. Second we are told to examine ourselves in the evening, and make sure that we have calmed down.

Conquering a hot temper is not achieved overnight but through prayer and the help of the Holy Spirit. We must remember that we cannot control how other people act or what they say we can only control how we respond back to them. When we don't allow anger to become rooted in our life we can respond in a way that will give God glory.

While proclaiming the promises of God about anger, we are reminded of how God wants us to exhibit self-control; not let anger disturb our Christian walk. Memorizing these Scriptures on anger is a fantastic way for self-reflection; they will allow God's Word to bring a peace that surpasses all understanding.

Prayer for Anger

Heavenly Father, I declare that in every situation I will pray, lifting holy hands without anger or quarreling. I pray for wisdom; to not be quick to get angry, because I realize anger lives in a fool's heart. I pray that I will have the strength to let all bitterness, wrath, anger, turmoil, and insult be put away from me. I pray that I will have the integrity to be quick to hear, slow to speak and slow to anger.

Father God, I pray that in my anger I will not sin or let the sun go down while I am still angry, so that I will not give the devil a foothold. I desire understanding, to control my anger; so that my foolish anger will not become immediately apparent but may I be levelheaded enough to overlooks an insult. I recognize that a hot-temper stirs up strife but when I am slow to anger it quiets arguments.

Holy Spirit, give me the discernment to not be friendly with angry people or keep company with hotheads who express their anger openly. I realize sensible people are patient and hold back their outburst but a bad temper is contagious and I don't want to get infected. I pray that I will have the common sense not to argue with angry people. Help me to remember that mockers can get a whole crowd agitated but the wise will calm anger.

In the mighty name of Jesus and by the authority He has given to me, I command the spirit of anger to release me. Amen.

Scriptures about Anger

"Let go of anger and leave rage behind! Don't get upset—it will only lead to evil." Psalm 37:8 CEB

"Be kind and compassionate to one another, forgiving each other, just as in Christ God forgave you." Ephesians 4:32 NIV

"And He looked around at them with anger, grieved at their hardness of heart, and said to the man, "Stretch out your hand." He stretched it out, and his hand was restored." Mark 3:5 ESV

"People with understanding control their anger; a hot temper shows great foolishness." Proverbs 14:29 NLT

"God is a righteous judge, and a God who feels indignation every day." Psalm 7:11 ESV

"Human anger does not produce the righteousness God desires." James 1:20 NLT

"In your anger do not sin" Do not let the sun go down while you are still angry. 27 and do not give the devil a foothold." Ephesians 4:26-27 NIV

"Let all bitterness and wrath and anger and clamor and slander be put away from you, along with all malice." Ephesians 4:31 ESV

"A soft answer turns away wrath, but a harsh word stirs up anger." Proverbs 15:1 ESV

"Insightful people restrain their anger; their glory is to ignore an offense." Proverbs 19:11 CEB

"Don't be too quick to get angry because anger lives in the fool's heart." Ecclesiastes 7:9 CEB

"Remember this, my dear brothers and sisters: Everyone should be quick to listen, slow to speak, and should not get angry easily. [20] An angry person doesn't do what God approves of." James 1:19-20 GW

"Better to get angry slowly than to be a hero; better to be even-tempered than to capture a city." Proverbs 16:32 GW

"Stupid people express their anger openly, but sensible people are patient and hold it back." Proverbs 29:11 GNT

"A hot-tempered man stirs up strife, but he who is slow to anger quiets contention." Proverbs 15:18 ESV

"The Lord is merciful and gracious; slow to anger and abounding in steadfast love." Psalm 103:8 ESV

"Don't hang out with angry people; don't keep company with hotheads. Bad temper is contagious—don't get infected." Proverbs 22:24 MSG

"And the Lord said do you do well to be angry?" Jonah 4:4 ESV

"A man without self-control is like a city broken into and left without walls." Proverbs 25:28 ESV

"If a wise man contend with a fool, whether he is angry or laugh, he shall find no rest." Proverbs 29:9 DRA

"A short-tempered man is a fool. He hates the man who is patient." Proverbs 14:17 TLB

"For My name's sake I defer My anger, for the sake of My praise I restrain it for you, that I may not cut you off." Isaiah 48:9 ESV

"Don't befriend angry people or associate with hot-tempered people." Proverbs 22:24 NLT

"Do not take revenge, dear friends, but leave room for God's wrath. For it is written, Vengeance belongs to Me I will pay them back, declares the Lord." Romans 12:19 NSV

"Be angry, and do not sin; ponder in your own hearts on your beds, and be silent." Selah Psalm 4:4 ESV

"Now, the effects of the corrupt nature are obvious: illicit sex, perversion, promiscuity, [20] idolatry, drug use, hatred, rivalry, jealousy, angry outbursts, selfish ambition, conflict, factions." Galatians 5:19-20 GW

"An angry person stirs up conflict, and a hot-tempered person commits many sins." Proverbs 29:22 NIV

"But now you must put them all away: anger, wrath, malice, slander, and obscene talk from your mouth." Colossians 3:8 ESV

"For the overseer must be blameless, as God's steward; not self-pleasing, not easily angered, not given to wine, not violent, not greedy for dishonest gain." Titus 1:7 WEB

"I desire then that in every place the men should pray, lifting holy hands without anger or quarreling." 1 Timothy 2:8 ESV

"A king's anger announces death, but a wise man makes peace with him." Proverbs 16:14 GWT

"Anger is cruel, and wrath is like a flood, but jealousy is even more dangerous." Proverbs 27:4 NLT

"But I say to you that everyone who is angry with his brother will be liable to judgment; whoever insults his brother will be liable to the council; and whoever says, 'You fool!' will be liable to the hell of fire." Matthew 5:22 ESV

"So in my anger I took an oath: 'They will never enter my place of rest." Hebrews 3:11 NLT

"The anger of a fool becomes readily apparent, but the prudent person overlooks an insult." Proverbs 12:16 ISV

"The anger of the Lord will not turn back until He has fully carried out His intended purposes. In days to come you will come to understand this." Jeremiah 30:24 NB

"You will say in that day: "I will give thanks to You, O Lord, for though You were angry with me, Your anger turned away, that You might comfort me." Isaiah 12:1 ESV

"Mockers can get a whole town agitated, but the wise will calm anger." Proverbs 29:8 NLT

"A person with great anger bears the penalty, but if you deliver him from it once, you will have to do it again." Proverbs 19:19 NB

"You forgave the guilt of the people and covered all their sins. Selah ³ You stopped all Your anger; You turned back from Your strong anger. You withdrew all Your wrath; You turned from Your hot anger." Psalm 85:2-3 NCV

"Love is patient, love is kind. It does not envy, it does not boast, it is not proud. ⁵ It does not dishonor others, it is not self-seeking, it is not easily angered, and it keeps no record of wrongs." 1 Corinthians 13:4-5 NIV

Chapter 3

Fear

God gives us all gifts and talents. So often we don't use them because we are letting fear rule us. Fear is an emotion brought on by a threat that may be real or made-up in our minds which causes a change in behavior, such as running away, hiding, or freezing. Fear triggers a chain reaction in the brain that starts with a stressful situation or thought and ends with the release of chemicals that can cause our heart to race, rapid breathing, and tighten muscles. Fear could occur in response to a specific situation happening in the present, or to a future situation, which is perceived as a danger to health, life, security, wealth, emotions or anything held precious.

Fear is a tool the Devil uses to make us miserable and destroy our peace. It's the common way that Satan attacks us.

Fear is the complete opposite of faith. God wants us to walk by faith and Satan wants us to walk by fear. When Jesus was faced with the Devil's lies and temptations, Jesus countered him with the truth of God's Word. Throughout Jesus' ministry He spoke the Word of God; He depended upon it to combat the trials He faced.

We will all encounter fear at some point in our life; whether they are big fears or little ones, real threats or just in our minds. Nevertheless, God wants to replace our fear with a confidence that comes from knowing who we really are in Christ. When we learn to live by faith, not letting fear rule our lives, we can live peacefully and joyfully. The Bible tells us in Proverbs 23:7, *As a man thinks in his heart, so is he.* We must remember where our minds go we will follow; since fear begins with a thought and then creates intense emotions that can rule us and lead us to live captured and full of distress.

God wants us to meditate on His Word so our minds can be renewed. The Bible tells us in Romans 12:2 *Don't become like the people of this world. Instead, change the way you think. Then you will always be able to determine what God really wants, what is good, pleasing, and perfect.* Practicing Godly meditation allows His Word to renovate our minds and it will become part of us. Reading the scripture over and over helps us to picture them in our mind then it will turn it into revelation and when we get revelation about something, the truth of it sets us free from the lie of the Enemy. We can have confidence as we read the Word and meditate on what God promises about us; our faith will grow and we will be able to speak His Word over the fears that torment us.

As soon as you are feeling fearful and need encouragement to overcome fear, make time to slowly read Scriptures on fear. I've learned that if my feelings or thoughts don't line up with God's Word, then what I feel and think is wrong and I quickly replace it with the truth of God's Word. Start today by making the decision to trust that God's Word is the truth. Then you will discover you can overcome your fears as you see yourself in Christ. Have faith that you will receive assurance from these fear-busting Scriptures.

Prayer for Fear

Heavenly Father, I declare even when I go through the darkest valley, I fear no danger, for You are with me; Your rod and Your staff they comfort me. Even when I am afraid, I still trust You. Thank You for not giving me a spirit of fear but one of power, love, and sound mind. I can confidently say the Lord is my helper and I will not be afraid of what anyone can do to me because if You are for me, who can be against me.

Holy Spirit, give me the ability to serve only God and fear Him alone; to obey His commands, listen to His voice, and cling to Him. Remind me that the angel of the Lord encamps around those who fear Him and He delivers them. I declare that the fear of the Lord leads to life, bringing security, and protection from harm; true humility and fear of the Lord leads to riches, honor, and long life.

Father God, I am certain, You alone are the one who comforts me, so I will not be afraid. I am so grateful that when I prayed to You Lord, You answered me and free me from all my fears. I declare that You are my light and my salvation, so I will not fear and You are my life's fortress, so I will not be afraid.

In the mighty name of Jesus, and by the authority He has given to me, I command the spirit of fear to release me. Amen.

Scriptures about Fear

"What can we say about all of this? If God is for us, who can be against us?" Romans 8:31GW

"For God has not given us a spirit of fearfulness, but one of power, love, and sound judgment." 2 Timothy 1:7 HCSB

"Even when I am afraid, I still trust You." Psalm 56:3 GW

"Oh, that they had such a heart in them that they would fear Me and always keep all My commandments, that it might be well with them and with their children forever!" Deuteronomy 5:29 NKJV

"Even though I walk through the dark valley of death, because You are with me, I fear no harm. Your rod and Your staff give me courage." Psalm 23:4 GW

"Do not be afraid, little flock, for your Father has been pleased to give you the kingdom." Luke 12:32 NIV

"So we can confidently say, The Lord is my helper. I will not be afraid. What can mortals do to me?" Hebrews 13:6 GW

"You must not fear them, for the Lord your God Himself fights for you." Deuteronomy 3:22 NKJV

"I know the plans that I have for you, declares the LORD. They are plans for peace and not disaster plans to give you a future filled with hope." Deuteronomy 3:22 NKJV

"The Lord is my light and my salvation. Who is there to fear? The LORD is my life's fortress. Who is there to be afraid of?" Psalm 27:1 GW

"The angel of the Lord encamps around those who fear Him, and He delivers them." Psalm 34:7 NIV

"Serve only the Lord your God and fear Him alone. Obey His commands, listen to His voice, and cling to Him." Deuteronomy 13:4 NLT

"Have I not commanded you? Be strong and courageous. Do not be frightened, and do not be dismayed, for the LORD your God is with you wherever you go." Joshua 1:9 ESV

"Love will never invoke fear. Perfect love expels fear, particularly the fear of punishment. The one who fears punishment has not been completed through love." 1 John 4:18 VOICE

"I praise God for what He has promised. I trust in God, so why should I be afraid? What can mere mortals do to me?" Psalm 56:4 NLT

"Like a bird protecting its young, God will cover you with His feathers, will protect you under His great wings; His faithfulness will form a shield around you, a rock-solid wall to protect you." Psalm 91:4-5 VOICE

"They do not fear bad news; they confidently trust the Lord to care for them. Do not tremble; do not be afraid." Psalm 112:7 NLT

"I alone am the one who comforts you. Why, then, are you afraid of mortals, who must die, of humans, who are like grass?" Isaiah 51:12 NOG

"Do not be afraid of them, for I am with you and will rescue you," declares the LORD." Jeremiah 1:8 NIV

"Jesus overheard what they were talking about and said to the leader, "Don't listen to them; just trust me." Mark 5:36 MSG

"But Jesus called to them, "It is I. Do not be afraid." John 6:20 NLV

"Don't be afraid," Moses answered them, "for God has come in this way to test you, and so that your fear of Him will keep you from sinning!" Exodus 20:20 NLT

"You must always act in the fear of the Lord, with faithfulness and an undivided heart." 2 Chronicles 19:9 NLT

"The secret of the Lord is for those who fear Him. And He will make them know His agreement." Psalm 25:14 NLV

"Yahweh's eyes are on those who fear Him, on those who wait with hope for His mercy." Psalm 33:18 NOG

"I prayed to the Lord, and He answered me. He freed me from all my fears." Psalm 34:4 NLT

"O fear the Lord, all you who belong to Him. For those who fear Him never want for anything." Psalm 34:9 NLV

"Like a father has compassion on His children, so Yahweh has compassion on those who fear Him." Psalm 103:13 WEB

"Fear of the Lord leads to life, bringing security and protection from harm." Proverbs 19:23 NLT

"True humility and fear of the Lord lead to riches, honor, and long life." Proverbs 22:4 NLT

"If you are afraid of people, it will trap you. But if you trust in the Lord, He will keep you safe." Proverbs 29:25 NIRV

"Charm is deceitful and beauty is passing, but a woman who fears the Lord, she shall be praised." Proverbs 31:30 NKJV

"He will be your sure foundation, providing a rich store of salvation, wisdom, and knowledge. The fear of the Lord will be your treasure." Isaiah 33:6 NLT

"Say to those with anxious heart, "Take courage, and fear not. Behold, your God will come with vengeance. The recompense of God will come, But He will save you." Isaiah 35:4 NASB

"Listen to me, you who know right from wrong you who cherish my law in your hearts. Do not be afraid of people's scorn, nor fear their insults." Isaiah 51:7 NLT

"Do not be afraid; you will not be put to shame. Do not fear disgrace; you will not be humiliated. You will forget the shame of your youth and remember no more the reproach of your widowhood" Isaiah 54:4 NIV

"For the Lord your God is living among you. He is a mighty savior. He will take delight in you with gladness. With His love, He will calm all your fears. He will rejoice over you with joyful songs." Zephaniah 3:17 NLT

"We have been rescued from our enemies so we can serve God without fear, in holiness and righteousness for as long as we live." Luke 1:74-75 NLT

"We faced conflict from every direction, with battles on the outside and fear on the inside. But God, who encourages those who are discouraged, encouraged us by the arrival of Titus. His presence was a joy." 2 Corinthians 7:5-6 NLT

"So let us be thankful, because we have a kingdom that cannot be shaken. We should worship God in a way that pleases Him with respect and fear." Hebrews 12:28 NCV

"Fear God," he shouted. "Give glory to Him for the time has come when He will sit as judge. Worship Him who made the heavens, the earth, the sea, and all the springs of water." Revelation 14:7 NLT

"And from the throne came a voice that said, "Praise our God, all His servants, all who fear Him, from the least to the greatest." Revelation 19:5 NLT

"Even though I walk through the darkest valley, I will fear no evil, for you are with me." Psalm 23:4 NIV

"Do not be afraid of anyone, for judgment belongs to God." Deuteronomy 1:17 NIV

"Do not be afraid of them. For the Lord your God is the one fighting for you." Deuteronomy 3:22 NLV

"The Lord is my light and my salvation— whom shall I fear? The Lord is the stronghold of my life— of whom shall I be afraid?" Psalm 27:1 NIV

"He said to His disciples, why are you so afraid? Do you still have no faith?" Mark 4:40 NIV

"Where God's love is, there is no fear, because God's perfect love drives out fear. It is punishment that makes a person fear, so love is not made perfect in the person who fears." 1 John 4:18 NCV

"Then He placed His right hand on me and said; do not be afraid. I am the First and the Last." Revelation 1:17 NIV

Chapter 4

Anxiety

We have all certainly experienced anxiety at some time in our lives. When we felt so preoccupied with a situation that we couldn't function or we've had an issue that seemed to take control of every waking thought so we could not sleep. Anxiety can be directly related to our sense of security. When life is going as planned and we feel safe in our daily routine, then anxiety subsides. On the other hand anxieties can increase when we feel threatened, insecure, or are overly consumed by something. Being concerned about things that might happen and being absorbed with something or troubled is not the same as anxiety. Anxiety is different from concern and uneasiness; anxiety is when our concerns become all-consuming and debilitating.

Some anxiety, without doubt, comes from the course of everyday life and that is normal; but intense, long-term, or frequent anxiety is harmful and can have a serious impact on our day-to-day life. Sometimes anxiety can get out of control, often with no obvious reason, exhibiting feeling of dread, fear, nervousness, apprehensive, or uneasiness of mind often over a future or anticipated event that might happen. An anxious person can show signs of sweating, tension, shaking, and increased pulse. Anxiety is also different from true fear because more often than not it is the result of an inward emotion rather than a reaction to an actual danger. Anxiety is one of the greatest thieves of joy.

The Bible tells us how to diminish anxiety in our lives, it says In Philippians 4:6, *Be anxious for nothing but in everything by prayer and supplication, with thanksgiving, let your requests be made known to God; and the peace of God, which surpasses all understanding, will guard your hearts and minds through Christ Jesus.* The Word of God is full of discernment and reassurance for those suffering from anxiety. Through studying the promises in God's Word we can learn to manage and overcoming our struggles with anxiety by understanding what the Bible says about them.

The Bible tells us to fight anxious thoughts by prayer and to pray about everything. We must realize that there is no trouble, event, situation, or circumstance that cannot be brought before the Father. Instead of talking to ourselves or to others we need to take our problems to someone who can help. We are told in Hebrews 4:16 *Let us then approach God's throne of grace with confidence, so that we may receive mercy and find grace to help us in our time of need.* Anxiety occurs when we try to face a situation ourselves relying upon our own strength rather than upon God and His Word. We must not forget that God can handle any problem.

Since life is full of countless surprises and there is no guarantee over our future, we can never be completely free from anxious thoughts. However when we put God first He will free us from anxiety and take care of our concerns. The first commandment God gave Moses was in Exodus 20:3, *You shall have no other gods before Me.* In other words, we should trust God first. When we choose to lean on our own understanding instead of God's promises we are choosing self-reliance instead of going to

God for His comfort. This can cause us to open our emotions to an overflow of anxiety, thinking over and over about what is bothering us.

The peace of God comes after we go to Him. We are told to go to God and make our appeal for a change in our situations; to not worry but to talk with the Lord who is near and to ask Him for what we need. We no longer have to be in control when we recognize that God is near to us and is listening to our requests. He knows what to do about our anxieties and He will bring us peace.

John 14:27 tells us, *I leave you peace. It is my own peace I give you. I give you pe*ace in a different way than the world does. So don't be troubled. The peace that Jesus gives should enable believers to remain calm in pain and trial. However the peace Jesus gives has to be received and applied in our lives. If we take hold of the promises of the peace of Christ, we will have calm, untroubled hearts, regardless of external circumstances.

Philippians 4:7 tells us, *And the peace of God, which surpasses every understanding, shall guard your hearts and your thoughts by Christ Jesus.* We have a troubled heart when we do not believe or trust His promise of peace. The peace of Christ is a great resource in helping us to know the will of God that is why we must depend on the peace of Christ. Naturally we sometimes fail in these areas. However, God is gracious and His help and peace is always available.

Discover how to live in peace by thinking about the Word and casting your cares upon Jesus. Nothing is more powerful than trusting God's Word to help during times filled with anxiety. As you read through the list of

Scriptures that promises you comfort and peace, find a few favorites and memorize them. Then when anxiety comes have faith in them; pray them back to God and thank Him in advance for setting you free from anxiety.

Prayer for Anxiety

Father God, I proclaim I will not be anxious about anything, but in every situation, by prayer and petition, with thanksgiving, I will present my requests to You. I am grateful that You are all around me on every side; You protect me with Your power. Your knowledge of me is too deep; it is beyond my understanding. You know when I sit or stand; when I am far away You know my every thought. You chart the path ahead of me and tell me where to stop and rest. I proclaim I will lie down in peace and sleep; for You alone will keep me safe.

Lord Jesus, thank You for leaving me with the gift of peace of mind and heart. I am certain the peace You give isn't like the peace the world gives, so I will not be troubled or afraid. I have confidence when I go through deep waters and great trouble, You will be with me.

Holy Spirit, help me to not let my heart be troubled, distressed, or nervous. Remind me that by being anxious I cannot add a single hour to my span of life; for that reason I will not be anxious about the anything. I pray that You will give me the courage to turn all my anxiety over to God because He cares for me.

In the mighty name of Jesus, and by the authority He has given to me, I command the spirit of anxiety to release me. Amen.

Scriptures about Anxiety

Then Jesus said, "Come to me, all of you who are weary and carry heavy burdens, and I will give you rest. Take my yoke upon you. Let me teach you, because I am humble and gentle, and you will find rest for your souls. For my yoke fits perfectly, and the burden I give you is light." Matthew 11:28-30 NLT

"And which of you by being anxious can add a single hour to his span of life?" Matthew 6:27 ESV

"I am leaving you with a gift--peace of mind and heart. And the peace I give isn't like the peace the world gives. So don't be troubled or afraid." John 14:27 NLT

"I will lie down in peace and sleep, for You alone, O Lord, will keep me safe." Psalm 4:8 NLT

"Turn all your anxiety over to God because He cares for you." 1 Peter 5:7 GW

"And I am sure that God who began the good work within you will keep right on helping you grow in His grace until His task within you is finally finished on that day when Jesus Christ returns." Philippians 1:6-7 TLB

"Therefore do not be anxious about tomorrow, for tomorrow will be anxious for itself. Sufficient for the day is its own trouble." Matthew 6:34 ESV

"Martha, Martha, you are anxious and troubled about many things." Luke 10:41 ESV

"An anxious heart weighs a man down, but a kind word cheers him up" Proverbs 12:25 NIV

"I sought the Lord, and He heard me; and He delivered me from all my troubles." Psalm 34:4 DRB

"You created every part of me; you put me together in my mother's womb." Psalm 139:13 GNT

"Do not be anxious about anything, but in every situation, by prayer and petition, with thanksgiving, present your requests to God." Philippians 4:6 NIV

"We know that God works all things together for good for the ones who love God, for those who are called according to His purpose." Romans 8: 28 CEB

"Never let yourself think that you are wiser than you are; simply obey the Lord and refuse to do wrong. [8] If you do, it will be like good medicine, healing your wounds and easing your pains." Proverbs 3:7-8 GW

"You are all around me on every side; You protect me with Your power. [6] Your knowledge of me is too deep; it is beyond my understanding." Psalm 139:1-23 GNT

"Be humbled, then, under the powerful hand of God, that you He may exalt in good time." 1 Peter 5:6 YTL

"I can endure all these things through the power of the one who gives me strength." Philippians 4:13 CEB

"Cast your burden upon the LORD and He will sustain you; He will never allow the righteous to be shaken." Psalm 55:22 NASB

"Trust in the Lord with all your heart. Never rely on what you think you know. ⁶ Remember the Lord in everything you do, and He will show you the right way." Proverbs 3:5-6 GW

"And the peace of God, that is surpassing all understanding, shall guard your hearts and your thoughts in Christ Jesus." Philippians 4:7 YLT

"I am at peace and even take pleasure in any weaknesses, insults, hardships, persecutions, and afflictions for the sake of the Anointed because when I am at my weakest, He makes me strong." 2 Corinthians 12:10 VOICE

"Therefore I tell you, do not worry about your life, what you will eat or drink; or about your body, what you will wear. Is not life more than food and the body more than clothes?" Matthew 6:25 NIV

"Examine me, O God, and know my mind; test me, and discover my thoughts." Psalm 139:33 GNT

"My God will meet your every need out of His riches in the glory that is found in Christ Jesus." Philippians 4:19 CEB

"And He said to His disciples, "Therefore I tell you, do not be anxious about your life, what you will eat, nor about your body, what you will put on. ²³ For life is more than food, and the body more than clothing. ²⁴ Consider the ravens: they neither sow nor reap, they have neither storehouse nor barn, and yet God feeds them. Of how much more value are you than the birds!" Luke 12:22-24 ESV

"May our Lord Jesus Christ Himself and God our Father, who loved us and in His grace gave us unfailing courage

and a firm hope, [17] encourage you and strengthen you to always do and say what is good." 2 Thessalonians 2:16-17 GNT

"Let go of your concerns! Then you will know that I am God. I rule the nations. I rule the earth." Psalm 46:10 GW

"Keep your lives free from the love of money, and be content with what you have because He has said, "I will never leave you; I will always be by your side." Hebrews 13:5 VOICE

"And which of you by being anxious can add a single hour to his span of life. [26] If then you are not able to do as small a thing as that, why are you anxious about the rest?" Luke 12:25-26 ESV

"Why am I so sad? Why am I so troubled? I will put my hope in God, and once again I will praise Him, my savior and my God." Psalm 42:5 GW

"In the same way, the Spirit comes to help our weakness. We don't know what we should pray, but the Spirit Himself pleads our case with unexpressed groans." Romans 8:26 CEB

"So as you can see, if I have to boast, I will, but only in my own weaknesses." 2 Corinthians 11:30 VOICE

"Lord, I am not proud and haughty. I don't think myself better than others. I don't pretend to "know it all." Psalm 131:1 TLB

"Many are the sorrows of the wicked, but he, who trusts in, relies on, and confidently leans on the Lord shall be compassed about with mercy and with loving-kindness." Psalm 32:10 AMP

"O Lord, you have examined my heart and know everything about me." Psalm 139:1 TLB

"Turn your burdens over to the Lord, and He will take care of you. He will never let the righteous person stumble." Psalm 55:22 GW

"If you will humble yourselves under the mighty hand of God, in His good time He will lift you up." 1 Peter 5:6-7 Living Bible TLB

"I will instruct you and teach you in the way you should go; I will counsel you with my eye upon you." Psalm 32:8 ESV

"When you go through deep waters and great trouble, I will be with you. When you go through rivers of difficulty, you will not drown! When you walk through the fire of oppression, you will not be burned up—the flames will not consume you." Isaiah 43:2-3 TLB

"God is our refuge and strength, a very present help in trouble." Psalm 46:1-11 ASV

"That is why we can say without any doubt or fear, "The Lord is my Helper, and I am not afraid of anything that mere man can do to me." Hebrews 13:6 TLB

"Do not let your hearts be troubled (distressed, agitated). You believe in and adhere to and trust in and rely on God; believe in and adhere to and trust in and rely also on Me." John 14:1 AMP

"You know when I sit or stand; when far away you know my every thought. ³ You chart the path ahead of me and tell me where to stop and rest. Every moment you know where I am." Psalm 139:2-3 TLB

"Be still, and know that I am God. I am exalted among the nations; I am exalted in the earth!" Psalm 46:10 RSV

Chapter 5

Depression

Depression is real and if you are fighting it you are not alone; it has touched many of life's great leaders in the Bible; Moses, Elijah, David, and Job all experienced depression. Most people have felt depressed at times. This feeling can be a common reaction to loss, struggles, or bruised self-esteem; it can include feelings of sadness, helplessness, hopelessness, and worthlessness. While medical and emotional problems often do contribute to depression, there may also be a spiritual Influence. Because we live in a world lacking hope, depression can be a spiritual outcome with a feeling of heaviness that pulls us down. The Word of God calls depression the spirit of heaviness and we are instructed in Isaiah 61:3, to Put on the garment of praise for the spirit of heaviness.

As Christians we can overcome depression when we take a hold of God's promises. God's Word provides a remedy that can help us move past depression. Proverbs 12:25 tells us that, Anxiety in the heart of man causes depression, but a good word makes it glad. We read here that a heart full of anxiety is the problem, but a good word is the cure. Jesus is the Word and the Word is the true cure for depression. Jesus has invited all to come to Him for the rest of our souls. We can have confidence that when we come to Jesus we will receive rest and obtain peace and comfort in our hearts.

Often depressed people find themselves swept into a whirlwind of self-involvement, which can keep them from loving themselves and others. That is why love is essential to overcome depression. God's Word teaches us in Luke 10:27 to, Love the Lord your God with all your heart, with all your soul, with all your strength, and with all your mind; and your neighbor as yourself. So often when depressed people begin to love the way the Scripture describes they are demonstrating true love and their depression begins to fade away.

We have been given the authority and responsibility to control our thoughts and bring them in line with the Word of God. 2 Corinthians 10:5 tells us, We pull down every proud obstacle that is raised against the knowledge of God; we take every thought captive and make it obey Christ. The Enemy watches and knows how and when to attack us; that is why we must take charge of what we think, watch, hear, see, and speak. Recognizing that Satan isn't afraid of our words, but he is afraid of God's Word is the first step to win the fight. Ephesians 6:17 tells us, Take the helmet of salvation and the sword of the Spirit, which is God's Word.

We have been given the sword of the Spirit, which is the Word of God. But the Word doesn't become our sword for us until we memorize it, speak it, and use it. Jesus defeated Satan in the wilderness, by responding with Scripture that He had already hidden in His heart.

The only thing that will truly destroy depression is God's hope and His Word is full of hope. These Scriptures on depression will help you to win the battle over depression; they will give you hope and restore your joy.

Start today to hide God's Word in your hearts by meditating, proclaiming, studying, and praying.

Prayer for Depression

Father God, it is the most amazing feeling to know how deeply You know me, inside and out; the realization of it is so great that I cannot comprehend it. How precious are Your thoughts about me, O God. They cannot be numbered. You are my source of hope; You fill me completely with joy and peace. You changed my sorrow into dancing. You took away my clothes of sadness and clothed me in happiness.

Lord Jesus, I am certain that You are near to those who are discouraged; You save those who have lost all hope. Thank You for allowing me to come to You when I am weary and carry heavy burdens; I am confident that You will give me rest. You comfort me in all my troubles so that I can comfort others.

Holy Spirit, encourage me to keep my thoughts on whatever is right or deserves praise: things that are true, honorable, fair, pure, acceptable, or commendable. Remind me when I trust the Lord I will become strong again. I will rise up as an eagle in the sky; I will run and not need rest; I will walk and not become tired.

In the mighty name of Jesus, and by the authority He has given to me, I command the spirit of depression to release me. Amen.

Scriptures about Depression

"The righteous call to the Lord and He listens; He rescues them from all their troubles. [18] The Lord is near to those who are discouraged; He saves those who have lost all hope." Psalm 34:17-18 GNT

"Then Jesus said, "Come to me, all of you who are weary and carry heavy burdens, and I will give you rest." Matthew 11:28 NLT

"Do not worry about anything but pray and ask God for everything you need, always giving thanks. [7] And God's peace, which is so great we cannot understand it, will keep your hearts and minds in Christ Jesus." Philippians 4:6-7 NCV

"Why, I ask myself, are you so depressed? Why are you so upset inside? Hope in God! Because I will again give Him thanks, my saving presence and my God." Psalm 43: 5 CEB

"The thief comes only to steal and kill and destroy; I have come that they may have life and have it to the full." John 10:10 NIV

"Give all your worries and cares to God, for He cares about you." 1 Peter 5:7 NLT

"Tell me in the morning about your love, because I trust You. Show me what I should do, because my prayers go up to You." Psalm 143:8 NCV

"Don't be afraid, for I am with you. Don't be discouraged, for I am your God. I will strengthen you and help you. I will hold you up with My victorious right hand." Isaiah 41:10 NLT

"Do not be shaped by this world; instead be changed within by a new way of thinking. Then you will be able to decide what God wants for you; you will know what is good and pleasing to Him and what is perfect." Romans 12:2 NCV

"He comforts us in all our troubles so that we can comfort others. When they are troubled, we will be able to give them the same comfort God Has given us." 2 Corinthians 1:4 NLT

"Distress that drives us to God does that. It turns us around. It gets us back in the way of salvation. We never regret that kind of pain. But those who let distress drive them away from God are full of regrets; end up on a deathbed of regrets." 2 Corinthians 7:10 MSG

"Finally, brothers and sisters, keep your thoughts on whatever is right or deserves praise: things that are true, honorable, fair, pure, acceptable, or commendable." Philippians 4:8 GW

"For His anger lasts only a moment, but His favor lasts a lifetime! Weeping may last through the night, but joy comes with the morning." Psalm 30:5 NLT

"Lord, answer me quickly, because I am getting weak. Don't turn away from me, or I will be like those who are dead." Psalm 143:7 NCV

"Trust the Lord with all your heart, and don't depend on your own understanding. ⁶ Remember the Lord in all you do, and He will give you success." Proverbs 3:5-6 NCV

"No, I will not abandon You or leave You as orphans in the storm—I will come to you." John 14:18 TLB

"He answered, "'Love the Lord your God with all your heart, with all your soul, with all your strength, and with all your mind. And love your neighbor as you love yourself." Luke 10:27 GW

"You changed my sorrow into dancing. You took away my clothes of sadness, and clothed me in happiness." Psalm 30:11NCV

"Search me, O God, and know my heart; test me and know my anxious thoughts." Psalm 139:23 NLT

"Blessed be the God and Father of our Lord Jesus Christ, the Father of mercies and God of all comfort; 2 Corinthians 1:3 WEB

"Don't you know that your body is a temple that belongs to the Holy Spirit? The Holy Spirit, whom you received from

God, lives in you. You don't belong to yourselves." 1 Corinthians 6:19 GW

"We share in the many sufferings of Christ. In the same way, much comfort comes to us through Christ." 2 Corinthians 1:5 ERV

"Even when we are weighed down with troubles, it is for your comfort and salvation! For when we ourselves are comforted, we will certainly comfort you. Then you can patiently endure the same things we suffer." 2 Corinthians 1:6 NLT

"How precious are Your thoughts about me, O God. They cannot be numbered! [18] *I can't even count them; they*

outnumber the grains of sand!   And when I wake up, You are still with me." *Psalm 139:17-18 NLT*

"The Lord defends those who suffer; He defends them in times of trouble." *Psalm 9:9NCV*

"A joyful heart makes a cheerful face, but when the heart is sad, the spirit is broken." *Proverbs 15:13 NASB*

"For I can do everything God asks me to with the help of Christ who gives me the strength and power."   *Philippians 4:13 TLB*

"It is the most amazing feeling to know how deeply You know me, inside and out; the realization of it is so great that I cannot comprehend it." *Psalm 139:6 VOICE*

"For the more we suffer for Christ, the more God will shower us with His comfort through Christ." *2 Corinthians 1:5 NLT*

"You were bought for a price. So bring glory to God in the way you use your body." *1 Corinthians 6:20 GW*

"Send Your light and truth—those will guide me! Let them bring me to Your holy mountain, to your dwelling place." *Psalm 43: 3 CEB*

"When life is dark, a light will shine for those who live rightly those who are merciful, compassionate, and strive for justice." *Psalm 112:4 VOICE*

"He lifted me out of the pit of destruction, out of the sticky mud. He stood me on a rock and made my feet steady." *Psalm 40:2 NCV*

"Worry weighs a person down; an encouraging word cheers a person up." Proverbs 12:25 NLT

"Spare me, Lord! Let me recover and be filled with happiness again before my death." Psalm 39:13 TLB

"Arise, shine; for your light has come, and Yahweh's glory has risen on you." Isaiah 60:1 WEB

"For she thought, "If I just touch His garments, I will get well." Mark 5:28 NASB

"I pray that God, the source of hope, will fill you completely with joy and peace because you trust in Him. Then you will overflow with confident hope through the power of the Holy Spirit." Romans 15:13 NLT

"But, Lord, You are my shield, my wonderful God who gives me courage." Psalm 3:3 NCV

"With perfect peace you will protect those whose minds cannot be changed, because they trust You." Isaiah 26:3 GW

"The Lord is the one who goes ahead of you; He will be with you. He will not fail you or forsake you. Do not fear or be dismayed." Deuteronomy 31:8 NASB

"You have surrounded me on every side, behind me and before me, and You have placed Your hand gently on my shoulder." Psalm 139:5 VOICE

"I told you these things so that you can have peace in me. In this world you will have trouble, but be brave! I have defeated the world." John 16:33 NCV

"As if that were not enough, because of Him my mind is clearing up. Now I have a new song to sing— a song of praise to the One who saved me. Because of what He's done, many people will see and come to trust in the Eternal." Psalm 40:3 VOICE

"Wicked people have many troubles, but the Lord love surrounds those who trust Him." Psalm 32:10 NCV

"He found them in a desert, a windy, empty land. He surrounded them and brought them up, guarding them as those He loved very much." Deuteronomy 32:10 NCV

"Even in the unending shadows of death's darkness, I am not overcome by fear." Because You are with me in those dark moments, near with Your protection and guidance, I am comforted." Psalm 23:4 VOICE

"But the people who trust the Lord will become strong again. They will rise up as an eagle in the sky; they will run and not need rest; they will walk and not become tired." Isaiah 40:31 NCV

Prayer of Salvation

Proclaiming Faith in Christ as Savior and Lord

God's grace He has already done everything to provide your salvation. Salvation is a gift from God. Ephesians 2:8 tells us, *For it is by grace you have been saved, through faith—and this is not from yourselves, it is the gift of God.* Your part is simply to believe and receive Jesus as your Lord and Savior. This is the most important decision you'll ever make. The prayer of salvation begins with faith in Jesus. When you're ready to become a Christian you'll have your first genuine conversation with God.

God's Word promises, in Romans 10:9-10, *If you declare with your mouth, "Jesus is Lord," and believe in your heart that God raised him from the dead, you will be saved. For it is with your heart that you believe and are justified, and it is with your mouth that you profess your faith and are saved.* You must believe that Jesus is God's one and only son. Believe that there are three persons in the Godhead the Father, the Son, and the Holy Spirit. Believe Jesus was crucified for your sins, was buried, rose from the dead, and ascended in to heaven. Believe that you receive salvation through the confession of and repentance from your sins. Believe that salvation is found in Jesus alone and there is no other name by which we can be saved. Ask Jesus to be your Lord and Savior.

If you believe then pray this prayer below out loud in faith and accept God's free gift.

Heavenly Father, I know that my sins have separated me from you. I am truly sorry. I am ready to walk away from my past sinful life and toward you. Please forgive me and help me avoid sinning again. I believe that Jesus is Your one and only son, that He died for my sins, and that You raised Him from the dead. By faith in Your Word, I invite Jesus to become the Lord of my life from this day forward. Please send your Holy Spirit to help me do Your will for the rest of my life. In Jesus' name I pray. Amen.

If you prayed this prayer and your repentance is sincere and your faith in Christ is genuine you are now a follower of Jesus, a child of God. God's Word promises that you are a new creation and your name is now written in the book of life.

Welcome to the family. I encourage you to find a church where you can be water baptized and grow in the knowledge of God through His Word, the Bible.

Send prayer request to: PrayerRequests@TerriFlynn.org

About the Author

Terri Flynn was born and raised in Kingston, New York. At age 12 a seed was planted in her heart that would slowly grow and mature to a passionate love for Christ. In 1999, she surrendered her life to Jesus and began to seek after God through fasting, prayer, and meditating on His promises. It was through these times of prayer and study that Terri discovered that God's promises apply to the spiritual, emotional, physical, and financial areas of her life.

A desire for the Word of God was rooted in Terri's life when she attended Spirit Vision Bible College; at which time she made a commitment to say yes to whatever God asked. She wholeheartedly believes in the Word of God and has a passion for praying and proclaiming His promises. She has faith that God has made promises to us in His Word and as believers we should trust His promises. Terri discovered the power to live victoriously by applying God's Word to her life and wants to support others to do the same. She published her first book God Delights in the Prayers of His Children, in 2013.

Terri is active in her local church, Free Chapel, and she considers it a privilege to serve as a volunteer. She believes that the blessings and talents she has been given should be used to bless others. She has served in children's, youth, marriage, women's, and the first steps prayer ministries, as well as other outreach ministries. She attended Spirit Vision Bible College, School of Discipleship, and Joy School of Ministry. She married Sean in 2007; they reside in Georgia with their blended family.

Enjoy this additional book from author Terri Flynn
God Delights in the Prayers of His Children
Praying God's Word Back to Him through Scripture-Based Prayer

Abridged Edition

God Promised
Proclaiming the Word Over

Volume Two

Joy, Love, Faith, Peace, and Kindness

Volume Three

Prayer, Fasting, Giving, Strength, and Finances

Available for purchase online and as e-book
(Prayer Book) https://www.createspace.com/5213557
(Volume 1) https://www.createspace.com/4926657
(Volume 2) https://www.createspace.com/5194452
(Volume 3) https://www.createspace.com/5213557
Visit me at: terriflynnauthor.weebly.com
https://www.facebook.com/PrayerRequestsTerriFlynn.org